Digital Marketing for Freelancers

Leveraging Social Media

Table of Contents

Your personal brand is a promise to your clients... a promise of quality, consistency, competency, and reliability.

— Jason Hartman

Chapter 1. Introduction

In this special report, we unlock the secret to becoming a successful freelancer by leveraging the power of social media. "Digital Marketing for Freelancers: Leveraging Social Media" is your comprehensive guide on how to use the digital world's influential tool to your advantage. This report is your key to the gateway where the art of marketing blends with the dynamic world of social media to create vast opportunities for freelancers. It's not about complex algorithms or hard-to-digest concepts; it's about making your mark in the digital world in the most simple, yet effective way. Discover how you can amplify your reach, build your brand and catapult your freelancing business to new heights. Be prepared to get inspired, invigorated and excited by the possibilities that await you. Let the journey to a successful freelancing career begin! Get your copy today and bring the change you've been waiting for!

Chapter 2. Understanding Digital Marketing: The Basics

Let us step into the world of digital marketing. Far from being an alien or intimidating entity, digital marketing is actually an umbrella term that encapsulates a myriad of strategies centered around promoting products or services through digital platforms. These digital platforms are where the majority of modern consumers spend their time: the internet, mobile phones, display advertising, and other digital mediums.

2.1. What is Digital Marketing?

Digital marketing is marketing accomplished through digital platforms. At the core of digital marketing lies connection — the connection between businesses or individuals (like freelancers) and their audience. Traditional marketing methods underutilize, or in some cases completely overlook some of these connections, thereby missing out on reaching potential customers.

Through advanced technologies and internet-based platforms these connections can be leveraged to reach a larger audience, converting potential customers into active consumers or clients. The power of these digital tools is manifold, but the fundamental idea remains the same: reach and engage audiences in a way that arouses interest and compels action.

2.2. The Importance of Digital Marketing

There's no denying the power and importance of digital marketing in today's digital world. The benefits are numerous. For freelancers, digital marketing offers a cost-effective way to promote their services, reach a larger audience, interact with potential clients, and build a brand that can stand tall amidst competition.

It's not an overstatement to say that digital marketing has levelled the playing field for individuals and small businesses to compete with larger corporations. For freelancers, this means no longer being overshadowed by big companies with deeper pockets. With effective digital marketing strategies, freelancers can emerge from obscurity, reaching a global audience without needing to invest exorbitant amounts.

2.3. Components of Digital Marketing

When it comes to the components of digital marketing, there are different facets to consider:

1. **Search Engine Optimization (SEO):** Often referred to as the backbone of digital marketing, SEO involves optimizing a website to improve its visibility on search engines. SEO is vital in positioning a website or a webpage at the top of search engine results pages (SERPs), thus increasing organic (non-paid) visits.

2. **Content Marketing:** This revolves around creating and distributing valuable, relevant, and consistent content with the aim of attracting and obtaining a defined audience.

3. **Social Media Marketing (SMM):** This involves leveraging social media platforms to connect, engage, and build relationships with the target audience. For freelancers, this is a vital tool for promoting your work to a large number of people at once.

4. **Email Marketing:** Email marketing is a form of direct marketing that uses emails to send promotional messages to a targeted group of people. It's useful for maintaining relationships with clients, promoting new offerings, and obtaining feedback.

5. **Pay-Per-Click (PPC):** A model of online marketing where advertisers pay a fee each time one of their ads is clicked. For freelancers, PPC can be an effective way to drive traffic to their online portfolio, blog, or website.

6. **Influencer Marketing:** The relatively new field of influencer marketing involves harnessing the power of influential personalities on social media. Freelancers can partner with influencers for cross-promotion and increased visibility.

2.4. Getting Started With Digital Marketing

As a freelancer beginning your digital marketing journey, it's easy to modernize your current approach. Start by identifying your target audience and setting clear goals. These can include boosting brand awareness, driving web traffic, or increasing client conversion rate. You can then choose the appropriate digital marketing techniques that will help you achieve these targets.

Fine-tune your online presence, including your website and social media profiles. Ensure that your communication remains consistent across all platforms. This includes using the same profile images, colors, and brand messaging.

Whether it's SEO, content marketing, SMM, email marketing, PPC, or a combination of these, choose methods that best resonate with your branding and audience. For instance, a writer may heavily lean on content and email marketing, while a graphic designer may focus on visual platforms and PPC.

Learning how to analyze your campaigns to derive insights is essential. It helps in the continuous improvement of your strategies and achieving your desired outcomes.

In conclusion, digital marketing is a powerful tool, especially for freelancers. A solid understanding of its basics is the first step in harnessing this power. Remember, digital marketing is not about quantity, but quality—quality of your audience, quality of your content, and ultimately, quality of the relationships you form through your digital marketing efforts.

Chapter 3. Laying the Freelance Foundation: Building Your Brand

The concept of a personal brand isn't a new one, but in the realm of digital freelancing it is crucial, as your brand serves as your calling card in the vast digital world. The essence of your brand isn't just about what service you provide, but also encompasses the unique qualities that set you apart and the values you wish to portray through your work.

3.1. Defining Your Brand Identity

The first and foremost step to building your brand is defining your identity. This is akin to crafting your own story; your personal narrative that forms the backbone of your brand. When defining your brand identity, consider the following aspects:

- What type of freelance work do you specialize in?
- What values do you consider important in your work?
- What unique qualities can you bring to the table?

While defining your identity, it's important to introspect and ask yourself these questions so that you have a clear vision about your brand. This clarity will guide you in making your decisions, from designing your logo and website to crafting your elevator pitch.

3.2. Creating Your Visual Identity

Once you've defined what you stand for, the next step is creating a visual representation of your brand. This should incorporate aspects such as color scheme, typography, and any other visual elements relevant to your brand. For instance, a freelancer specializing in environmental consulting might choose earth tones and natural images, while a graphics designer may opt for bold colors and innovative designs. The goal is to match your visuals to the personality and ethos of your brand.

3.3. Crafting Your Brand's Voice

Your brand's voice, like the visual identity, should be an authentic representation of your personality and values. It should resonate with your target audience and build a connection with them. Reflect on how you want to communicate with your audience. Will your brand speak with formal tone or a casual one? Will it be humorous or serious? Every word, sentence, and paragraph you communicate should align with your brand's voice.

3.4. Establishing Your Online Presence

With your brand's identity, visuals, and voice in place, it's time to establish your online presence. Start by setting up profiles on relevant social media platforms. Whether it's LinkedIn, Twitter, Facebook, or Instagram, each platform offers unique opportunities to reach and engage with your target audience. However, be mindful of your choice of platform; it should align with both your brand and your audience's preferences.

Your website is another key element of your online presence. It should not only showcase your portfolio, but also reflect your brand's identity and tell your brand's story. Remember, your website is often the first point of contact for potential clients, so make the most of it!

3.5. Continuously Refining Your Brand

Building your brand is not a one-time activity; it's a continuous process. As you grow and evolve as a freelancer, so too should your brand. Regularly review and refine your brand to ensure it stays true to your values, accurately represents your work, and continues to resonate with your target audience.

Remember, your brand is more than just a static logo or catchy tagline. It's a living, evolving entity that encapsulates your unique identity, value proposition, and freelance journey. It is your reputation in the digital marketplace, it's the promise you offer to your clients, and ultimately, it is the cornerstone of your freelance career.

Building a strong, authentic brand is no easy task. It requires a deep understanding of who you are, what you do, and why you do it, as well as a vigilant eye on the evolving trends and expectations in the digital world. But once established, your brand can be your greatest asset, helping you stand out in the crowded digital landscape, attract ideal clients, and pave the way for a successful freelancing career.

Chapter 4. Social Media Platforms: An Overview for Freelancers

The concept of social media, while seemingly ubiquitous today, is actually a relatively recent development within the context of human history. The global platform opens doors to a plethora of communication channels, allowing for instantaneous interactions across vast geographical boundaries. It leverages the art of digital storytelling to create a global village where brands can interact with consumers in real-time, and freelancers can effortlessly reach potential clients.

Before delving into the specifics of these platforms and how they can aid in your freelancing journey, we need to clearly define what social media is. At its core, social media represents both a collective and an individual space. Collectively, it serves as a hub for groups, organizations, and individuals to share ideas, thoughts, and perspectives. On the individual side, it provides a space where users build and curate their unique presence, connecting with like-minded individuals and potentially creating professional opportunities. Each social media platform has its own distinctive characteristics, uses, audience, and capabilities, and understanding these nuances is critical to leveraging them successfully.

4.1. The Dominant Players: Facebook, Instagram, LinkedIn, and Twitter

Let's kick off with some of the most popular platforms freelancers should consider using as part of their social media strategy.

Facebook, with its billions of users, allows businesses and freelancers to create pages dedicated to their professional pursuits. Using this platform, you can interact with potential clients, share content related to your services, and create targeted advertisements to attract leads. Facebook Groups also provide a space for focused, communal discussion, enabling you to network with potential clients or connect with your peers.

Instagram, another powerhouse in the social media landscape, provides a visually-oriented platform perfect for those whose work often produces beautiful visual results – photographers, designers, artists, and the like. An Instagram business profile offers access to insights and analytics, a contact button, and the ability to promote posts, allowing you to take your freelance work to the next level.

LinkedIn is the premier social networking site for professionals. It's the perfect platform for freelancers to build professional relationships, connect with potential clients, and showcase their portfolio. The platform's news feed is also a great way to stay current with industry advancements and trends, and its thought leadership feature makes it easier to boost your professional credibility and reputation within your network.

Twitter serves as a microblogging site that allows users to post succinct thoughts known as 'tweets.' For freelancers, Twitter can serve as an announcement board of sorts for their services and updates. It can also be a fantastic place for immediate, succinct engagement with followers and potential clients.

4.2. Niche Platforms: Pinterest, Tumblr, and Snapchat

While the aforementioned platforms might seem like obvious choices for your freelancing business, don't overlook niche social media platforms.

Pinterest, primarily driven by visual content, allows users to 'pin' images or links to their own curated boards. Freelancers, particularly those with visually engaging content, can utilize Pinterest as an aesthetically pleasing portfolio that directs potential clients to their website or blog.

Tumblr, a blogging site, is more popular among the younger demographic and enjoys a strong presence of creatives. Depending on your target demographics and the nature of your services, Tumblr can be a great place to share your work and ideas, and interact with potential clients in a more casual, creative environment.

Snapchat provides a platform for sharing short, temporary videos and pictures known as 'snaps.' Though not every freelancer might find Snapchat beneficial, it can be a fun, casual way to draw a younger crowd and showcase a 'behind-the-scenes' look at your freelance work.

4.3. Understanding Your Audience and Choosing the Right Platforms

While the plethora of social media platforms can seem overwhelming, it's crucial to remember that less is more. Spreading yourself too thin across an array of platforms often dilutes your online presence and leaves little room for quality engagement.

Understanding your audience, as well as the nature of your freelance services, should be the primary drivers behind your choice of platforms. Are you primarily B2B or B2C? Engaging with young millennials or seasoned professionals? Is your work visual or text-driven? Knowing the answers to these questions will guide you towards the platforms that best suit your freelancing brand and audience.

In summary, social media is an exceptionally versatile tool that can be tailored to the unique needs and goals of your freelancing business. It enables you to connect and engage with potential clients more efficiently, showcase your work, and build a community around your brand – all vital elements to thriving in the freelance landscape. With a clear understanding of each platform's features and audience, coupled with a well-articulated strategy, you'll be well-equipped to unlock the potential of social media for your freelance business.

Chapter 5. Creating Engaging Content: The Fuel for Your Social Media Engine

Content is the bedrock of any social media marketing campaign. In essence, it is the fuel that powers your social media engine, propelling you forward in the crowded digital landscape. It's the story you tell, the information you disseminate, and the dialogues you facilitate. But not just any content will do. Producing outstanding content that is engaging, useful, and shareable is essential.

5.1. Understanding Engaging Content

At its simplest, engaging content is any type of material that inspires your audience to interact. These interactions can take multiple forms, including likes, shares, comments, or clicks on your posts. So, what does this tell us about content? Primarily, it must resonate with the audience. It must make them feel something, answer a question, or provide value that triggers them to engage.

Engaging content is crafted with the audience in mind. It addresses their pain points or interests, provides solutions, educates, entertains, or inspires. Therefore, as a freelancer, understanding your audience should be the cornerstone of any content creation process. Once you understand your audience's interests and needs, you can create content tailored to them, enhancing the likelihood of engagement.

5.2. Employing Variety in Content Types

One of the secrets of creating engaging content lies in variety. Different types of content appeal to the varying interests of your audience, and mixing it up can keep your content feed feeling fresh and exciting.

Image Posts are popular on all social media platforms. They are eye-catching, easy to consume, and perfect for visual storytelling.

Videos have soared in popularity in the recent years and are statistically one of the most engaging content types. A well-made video can be incredibly effective at conveying complex information in an accessible and engaging way.

Infographics are a visually attractive way to present complex information or data concisely and attractively.

Blog posts/Articles are perfect for providing in-depth information or insights on a particular topic. They help build thought leadership and credibility.

Interactive content such as polls and quizzes are great for deeper audience involvement.

User-generated content is another powerful way to engage your audience, as it directly involves them in your content creation.

5.3. Crafting Engaging Written Content

Engaging content is as much about how you write as what you write. Below are some tried-and-tested tips to create compelling written content:

- Use a Conversational Tone: The tone of your writing should reflect the way you would speak to your audience in person; conversational, human, and authentic.

- Simple Language: Avoid complex language and jargons. Your purpose is to communicate, not just to impress.

- Use Headlines and Sub-Headers: These break up your text and make it easier to read and comprehend.

- Tell a Story: Storytelling is a powerful way to engage your audience emotionally. It can make your content more memorable and impactful.

- Call to Action: Guide your audience on what to do next. Encourage them to comment, like, share, or visit your website or blog.

5.4. Leveraging Visuals for Engagement

Humans process visuals 60,000 times faster than text. Images stimulate emotions and can communicate complex concepts faster. Hence, integrating relevant images, videos, infographics, and other visual aids significantly improves engagement.

When creating visuals, ensure that they align with your overall brand aesthetic. Consistence in color schemes, style and quality boosts your brand recognition. Also, always ensure that your visuals are optimized for each specific social media platform.

5.5. Content Optimization for Engagement

Just creating engaging content is not enough. You must optimize it to be discoverable and shareable. Place your primary keywords strategically in your content without disrupting natural flow, include relevant hashtags, tag influencers or persons mentioned and include share buttons.

Also, consider timing of content. Ensure your content is published when your audience is most likely active for maximum engagement.

Social media is a bustling engine that's ready to churn out opportunities for those who know how to harness its potential. Your content is the fuel that sets this engine running. Hence, mastering the art of creating engaging content is an instrumental skill for freelancers venturing into the world of social media marketing.

Chapter 6. Importance of SEO and Keywords in Digital Marketing

The optimization of the search engine, known as Search Engine Optimization or SEO, and the careful selection of keywords play crucial roles in digital marketing, so they warrant considerable attention.

6.1. The Basics of SEO

SEO is a technique for increasing the quantity and quality of traffic visiting your website through organic search engine results. Organic search results are unpaid and are generally more trusted by users because they are based on relevance to the search query, not on paid promotion.

SEO involves understanding how search engines such as Google, Bing, and Yahoo function and how you can optimize your website content to appear in top search results. There are hundreds of factors that these platforms use to rank the results, most of which remain trade secrets.

Good SEO practices include providing valuable, high-quality content on your website, ensuring a fast load time, using meta descriptions and tags correctly, and ensuring that your website is easy to navigate, among others. SEO is not a one-time effort but requires continuous work, monitoring, and tweaking.

6.2. Keywords and Their Significance

Keywords in digital marketing are specific words or phrases that potential clients use to search for products, services, or content online. They are the bridge between what people are looking for and the content you provide to fill that need.

For freelancers specifically, it's crucial to understand what keywords are relevant to your services, industry, and target market. By investigating and selecting appropriate keywords, you can optimize your digital content effectively, making it easier for your prospective clients to find you.

Optimizing your content with relevant keywords helps search engines understand what your website is about, subsequently increasing your visibility in search engine results.

6.3. SEO and Content Creation

When producing a piece of content, SEO needs to be considered from the beginning. This includes:

- Planning around a select group of relevant keywords.

- Organizing structured content (using headers, bullet points, and proper paragraphs for easy scanning).

- Using SEO-friendly URLs (short and relevant).

- Adding alt tags to images used in your content.

- Including both internal and external links to boost SEO.

- Regularly updating your content so search engines see your website as fresh and relevant.

Tailoring your content to SEO practices is not about stuffing it with keywords but about producing beneficial, engaging content for your visitors that also targets the most vital aspects considered by search engines.

6.4. The Power of Long-Tail Keywords

Focusing on more specific, often longer terms known as long-tail keywords can be a highly effective strategy. For instance, instead of focusing on 'freelance writer', use 'freelance tech writer for software companies'. The competition for these is typically lower, making it easier for your content to rank. These keywords often indicate more intent from the user and can often lead to higher conversion rates.

6.5. SEO Tools and Keyword Research

There is a range of tools, both free and paid, that can aid in your SEO efforts and keyword research. Google Keyword Planner, SEMrush, Moz, and Ubersuggest are some popular examples. These tools can provide key insights such as search volumes, competition levels, related keywords, and more, making your SEO efforts more data-driven.

6.6. Monitoring SEO Performance

After implementing SEO strategies, it's integral to monitor your website's performance and make necessary adjustments. Google Analytics and Google Search Console are excellent tools for this, providing valuable insights into your website's traffic, how users found your website, the performance of specific pages, and more.

SEO and well-selected keywords, when correctly harnessed, can elevate the visibility and impact of your digital content. Remember, SEO is not a get-rich-quick scheme but a long-term strategy. It's not about tricking search engines but about providing valuable content that improves a user's online experience. With consistent effort and smart strategies, you can improve your online presence and reach your ideal clients more efficiently.

Chapter 7. Building Your Online Presence: Social Media Strategies for Freelancers

Building a formidable online presence carries the power to influence your freelance career significantly. The digital age offers numerous channels; however, knowing how to leverage these channels in the manifold of social media spectrum is the key. Let's delve into the nitty-gritty of building and enhancing your online presence as a freelancer, employing effective social media strategies.

7.1. Understanding Social Media Algorithm

Virtually all social media platforms are guided by an algorithm. These algorithms technically function to present the most relevant content to each user. From a freelancer's perspective, understanding how these algorithms work forms the foundation of any sound social media strategy.

The algorithm is usually oriented around Engagement, Relevance, and Recency. Engagement entails the number of likes, comments, shares, and views a post generates. Relevance deals with how pertinent the algorithm believes your post might be to the user based on their interaction history. Recency refers to the freshness of your content; newer content often gets priority.

By understanding these elements, you can craft your social media posts strategically to meet the favors of the algorithm, leading to better visibility of your content.

7.2. Developing a Consistent Personal Brand

Your personal brand is essentially how clients perceive you. It's crucial to define your brand personality and reflect that consistently across all your social media platforms. Make sure that your brand embodies your unique selling proposition (USP), mission, values, and personality. It is essential to stay coherent and consistent with these elements in all your posts, interactions, and connections.

To make your brand "feel" tangible, consider elements like a consistent color scheme, logo, tone of voice in posts, and the overall visual layout of your profiles. Keep these synchronized across platforms to result in enhanced recognition and a professional appeal.

7.3. Content Strategy: Provide Value Regularly

Creating engaging, valuable content is a surefire way to attract and retain potential clients. Your content should be tailored according to the interests and needs of your target audience. The more valuable your content is, the more likely it will generate engagement, thereby enhancing your online presence.

Plan your content in advance for regular posting. Create a wide array of content including blogs, videos, tweets, Instagram photos, infographics or LinkedIn articles depending on the platforms you're active on. This will not only showcase your broad skill range but also keep your audience engaged and waiting for more.

7.4. Make Use of Stories, Live Streams, and Videos

Engagement and recency favor algorithms, both of which you can tap into by using "Stories," "Live Streams," and short-format videos that are now popular across most platforms. Live interactions provide real-time engagement, fostering a sense of community among your followers. Such forms of content can help you demonstrate a more authentic side of your brand, creating stronger bonds with your audience.

7.5. Engaging With Your Audience and Influencers

Interaction is the essence of social media platforms. Engaging with your audience makes them feel valued and helps in building loyal followers. Always respond to comments, messages, or emails in a timely and professional manner.

Connecting with influencers or major players in your industry will help you to gain access to their follower base as well. Don't shy away from collaborations, shout-outs, or even a friendly conversation. Remember, your network is your net worth in the social media world.

7.6. Scheduled Posting and Analytics

Be consistent and timely with your posts. Each platform has 'peak' times when your audience is most active. Scheduling your posts for these peak times ensures maximum visibility.

Ensure you monitor your progress using the analytics tools provided by these platforms. It's a treasure trove of data at your disposal, revealing much about your followers and how they interact with your content. Utilize this data to continually refine your strategies.

Remember, building an online presence takes time, and it's more of a marathon than a sprint. Keep experimenting with different strategies, but always base your decisions on data rather than mere instinct. Be patient, be persistent, and soon the power of social media will start working in your favor. Keep refining your strategies, keep learning, and keep evolving. Success on social media mirrors success in freelancing: it's an ongoing journey rather than a final destination.

Chapter 8. Effective Communication and Networking Through Social Media

The advent of social media has metamorphosed the way freelancers communicate and network. This communication is not just limited to their immediate community but extends to connect with millions of potential clients and collaborators around the world. It's redefining how relationships are built and maintained in the virtual space. This chapter is dedicated to improving your dexterity in communicating effectively and leveraging the networking capabilities of different social media platforms.

8.1. Understanding the Essence of Communication

Effective communication on social media is not merely spewing words. It is about delivering your message in a strategic, engaging, and interactive manner. This means articulating your thoughts clearly and engagingly but also interpreting and responding appropriately to your audience's feedback. This bi-directional process demands constant attention, improvisation, and a bit of creativity.

8.2. Crafting the Right Message

Crafting effective messages requires an understanding of your audience. Knowing their interests, preferences, and traits can help tailor your content accordingly. Employ empathy and emotional intelligence to resonate with your audience. Your message should be clear, succinct, precise, and easily comprehensible. Use simple language to make your content inclusive.

8.3. The Art of Listening on Social Media

Social media is not merely about talking; it's also about listening. Being attentive to your audience's perspectives, opinions, and responses to your posts provides valuable insights. This can help you adjust your strategy, content, and mode of communication. Follow your audience's conversations, discussions, and trends closely to stay attuned to their needs and expectations.

8.4. Building Long-lasting Relationships

Social media provides opportunities to build meaningful relationships with potential clients, colleagues, and mentors. Engaging with people's posts, addressing their concerns, and showing appreciation for their work helps in forging strong bonds. It's important to respond promptly to messages and comments. Remember, building relationships is a continuous process and demands consistency and patience.

8.5. Harnessing the Power of Networking

Networking on social media platforms can expand your horizons and open up several opportunities. Joining relevant groups and forums can help you collaborate with likeminded individuals and gain visibility. Consistently sharing valuable content, attending virtual events, and engaging in meaningful online dialogue helps establish your presence and credibility.

8.6. Leveraging Different Social Media Platforms

Each social media platform presents unique networking opportunities. LinkedIn, for instance, is a professional platform ideal for networking, finding clients, and sharing niche-specific content. Twitter, on the other hand, can be used for quick updates, sharing news, and participating in trending conversations. Instagram and Pinterest are great for visually driven content, while Facebook can reach a diverse audience base.

8.7. Balancing Professionalism and Personal Touch

While it's essential to maintain professionalism on your social media profiles, introducing elements of your personality can make your interactions more relatable and engaging. Post about your hobbies, interests, and leisure activities occasionally to strike a balance. Showcasing authenticity while maintaining appropriate boundaries can help sustaining fulfilling relationships.

8.8. Navigating Social Media Etiquettes

Knowing and adhering to the unwritten rules of social media etiquette is vital. Be respectful in your interactions, abstain from hateful speech, avoid getting too personal, and don't forget to credit sources when necessary. Manage conflicts with grace and learn from your mistakes.

By mastering effective communication and leveraging the power of networking on social media, you can promote your freelancing business, build a loyal and engaged following, and establish yourself as an authority in your field. Though this process requires time and consistency, the benefits of these practices are both considerable and enduring. This chapter is your stepping-stone to engaging more effectively with the online world and reaping the rewards from the same, helping you to elevate the trajectory of your freelancer journey.

Chapter 9. Utilizing Paid Social Media Marketing: When and How

In the vast pantheon of social media marketing strategies, paid marketing holds a critical position. These strategies help freelance digital marketers provide their businesses with an almost unfettered access to potential clients. But the question is: when should you utilize it, and how? In this section, we will explore that very notion, digging deep into the core principles and practical considerations of leveraging paid media marketing.

9.1. When to Use Paid Social Media Marketing

The decision to engage in paid social media marketing is often determined by several unique factors. First and foremost is the necessity to bolster organic marketing efforts. If your organic social media strategies don't generate the desired networking opportunities or engagement, a well-placed investment in paid marketing might just swing the momentum in your favor.

One key aspect to consider is the maturity stage of your freelancing business. New freelancers trying to make a place for themselves in an already saturated market can benefit from paid marketing's quick results. Established freelancers seeking to expand their clientele might also seek the advanced targeting capabilities that paid marketing provides.

Furthermore, specific goals or campaigns can warrant the use of paid marketing. For instance, when launching a new service, showcasing a portfolio, or announcing a partnership with a prominent client, you might want to ensure a certain level of visibility which can be achieved through paid social media marketing.

9.2. How to Use Paid Social Media Marketing

After identifying when to utilize paid marketing, the next step is understanding how to do so effectively. With an array of platforms available, each offering its unique environment and audience, mastering this art can be a bit overwhelming.

The first step is to set clear and specific objectives for your paid campaign. Knowing what you aim to achieve—be it increased website traffic, brand visibility, lead generation, or direct conversions—will shape the choice of platform, ad creative, budget, and targeting strategies.

Once you have your objectives in place, choose the social media platform based on where your target audience mostly resides. For instance, Facebook and Instagram are helpful for reaching a broad demographic, while LinkedIn is more suited to targeting professionals and businesses.

Next, identify and segment your target audience for each campaign. Detailed customer personas can be invaluable here, providing the likes, dislikes, behavior, and demographic data that underpin successful ad targeting. Use these insights to fine-tune your placements and ensure that your content resonates deeply with its intended recipients.

Developing creative and engaging ad content is the heart of your campaign. Experiment with various ad formats (image, video, carousel, stories, etc.) available across different platforms and invest in well-written copy and high-quality visuals.

Defining a budget is an equally important task. It can be a fixed amount per campaign or a daily/weekly/monthly cap. Keep in mind that higher budget doesn't always promise better results. Hence, it's crucial to monitor and optimize your campaigns periodically.

Optimization involves analyzing campaign performance and making necessary adjustments to maximize return on investment. This might mean tweaking your ad creative, targeting settings, or budget based on data feedback.

9.3. Conclusion

In conclusion, the use of paid social media marketing is a strategic business decision dictated by business maturity, market circumstances, and specific campaign goals. Execution involves diligent planning and consistent review, involving setting clear objectives, identifying the right audience, creating captivating content, outlining budgets, and frequent optimization based on performance metrics. By understanding and implementing these steps, freelancers can make the most of the paid social media landscape, using it to formulate a pivotal component of their marketing symbiosis and securely establishing their presence amidst niche visibility. Be it a seasoned freelancer or a budding enthusiast, paid social media marketing holds a wealth of untapped potentials, waiting to be harnessed.

Chapter 10. Evaluating Success: Metrics and Analytics in Social Media Marketing

As freelancers wade through the ocean of digital marketing, mastering the power of social media to enhance their brand's visibility, understanding the concept and importance of measuring success cannot be overstated. Equipped with tools of the digital age like metrics, analytics, and data, the world of social media marketing provides freelancers with a platform that allows them to measure the success (or otherwise) of their marketing efforts, and tweak them as necessary. This ongoing formative assessment is as crucial as it is endless, and is underscored by clarity of vision, meticulous planning, and sound strategy development.

10.1. Understanding Metrics and Analytics

Beginners in the field of social media might wonder what's meant by metrics and analytics. In simplest terms, metrics are measurements. They represent the hard numbers associated with content or activity on social media. Examples include the number of followers on your page, the number of likes your post has received, or the number of times your content was shared. Essentially, the "what" of the data.

Meanwhile, analytics delves deeper, unearthing the "why" behind the metrics. Analytics involves interpreting these metrics, looking at patterns, trends, and changes over time, allowing an understanding of the behavior and preferences of your audience which can be used to refine your social media marketing strategy.

10.2. The Importance of Selecting the Right Metrics

A fundamental element of your social media marketing strategy is consciously choosing the metrics you intend to monitor. These chosen key performance indicators (KPIs) must align perfectly with your defined social media goals. For instance, if your goal focuses on brand awareness, monitoring metrics like reach, followers count, or impressions will be beneficial. If your aim is to improve conversion rates, closely observing metrics such as click-through rates, conversion rates, or leads generated would be the most logical approach.

10.3. Tracking Engagement

One of the most important metrics to assess in social media marketing is 'Engagement.' This indicates how interactive your audience is with your content. This could include likes, shares, comments, and retweets on platforms like Facebook, Instagram, LinkedIn, and Twitter. This metric signifies your content's ability to captivate and engage your audience, making this a critical performance yardstick.

10.4. Conversion Rate Analysis

Monitoring your conversion rate tells you how successful your content is at guiding users to perform desired actions. Depending on your specific business goal, conversions could be as simple as a user clicking the link in your bio, or as major as a client booking your freelance services through your social media platform. By analyzing your conversion rate, you gain deeper insights into the efficacy of your content and how compelling it is to your audience.

10.5. Using Social Media Analytics Tools

There's an array of tools available to freelancers for analyzing their social media performance. Platform-specific options, such as Facebook Insights or Twitter Analytics, render easy-to-comprehend graphical representations of your data. For more granular, detailed analyses, you might resort to third-party tools like Buffer, Hootsuite, or Sprout Social that not only evaluate performance but also aid in content management and scheduling.

10.6. The Connection Between Metrics, Analytics and Ever-evolving Marketing Tactics

A deep-seated understanding of social media metrics and analytics allows you to adapt to your constantly changing environment. As trends shift and algorithms evolve, being able to pivot efficiently can be the difference between falling flat or successfully riding the wave. Choosing the right metrics, employing the appropriate analytics tools, and understanding what these numbers mean for your freelancing business are defining elements in your pursuit of social media success.

By amalgamating metrics and analytics, following a disciplined approach, continuously optimizing your strategy based on your data's story, you can open vistas of opportunities for yourself not previously imaginable. Remember, this isn't a numerical game; it's indeed a strategic voyage. Daunting though it may seem, embracing social media metrics and analytics and integrating them into your marketing strategy can lead to a profound, positive impact on your freelance career.

Chapter 11. The Art of Staying Relevant: Continuous Learning in Digital Marketing

Starting your journey in the world of digital marketing as a freelancer can seem quite daunting. There's so much to learn, and the landscape changes so rapidly, it can feel overwhelming just trying to keep up. Yet staying relevant and continuously learning is not just an option, it's a survival strategy in this dynamic field. Let's delve further into the art of maintaining relevancy and commitment to ongoing education in digital marketing.

11.1. The Ever-changing Landscape of Digital Marketing

The nature of the internet is such that it is always in a constant state of flux and evolution. Each day, new trends emerge, old ones die out, and algorithms are updated. There is a never-ending stream of new applications, platforms, features, techniques, and tools being unveiled. These factors make it crucial for any digital marketer to stay updated, adaptable and flexible. If you fail to do so, you run the risk of employing outdated practices which not only fail to yield results but could also negatively impact your online presence.

11.2. The Importance of Continuous Learning

The principle of lifelong learning is an essential asset in a digital marketer's toolkit. Every piece of new information or skill you acquire opens new doors of opportunities and enhances your ability to execute successful marketing campaigns. The knowledge enhances your strategies, boosts your problem-solving abilities, and provides you with more options when planning your campaigns. This continuous learning also improves your market value, making you highly sought after by clients.

11.3. Strategies for Staying Updated

With the vast amount of information available on the internet, it can be challenging to figure out what's worth your time and what's not. Here are some strategies that you may find helpful for continuous learning in digital marketing.

1. Subscribe to reputable marketing blogs and newsletters: Blogs like Moz, HubSpot, and Copyblogger regularly publish useful content related to digital marketing.

2. Follow thought leaders on social media: Thought leaders are people who are experts in digital marketing and are often the first to know about any new developments. Following them gives you access to this knowledge.

3. Attend webinars and workshops: These provide practical insights that can help you improve your own marketing strategies.

4. Read books about digital marketing: Though the field is ever-changing, there are some basics which remain the same. Books help you gain a deep understanding of these principles.

5. Join online communities: Digital marketing communities such as those on Reddit or Quora offer immeasurable help with real-time advice, insights, and discussions on the latest trends.

11.4. Making Learning a Habit

In order to maintain continuous learning, it's important to make it a regular habit. Set aside time each day to catch up on industry news or to learn a new skill. A commitment to daily learning helps to keep the mind fresh and open to new ideas. This habit also ensures that you steadily improve your knowledge without feeling a sense of overwhelm. Remember, the goal is not to know everything all at once, but rather to steadily and consistently increase your knowledge and skills.

11.5. Adapting to Change

Your ability to adapt to changes in the landscape is what will set you apart in digital marketing. When new information presents itself, having an adaptable mindset will enable you to assess the potential impact and make the necessary adjustments in your strategies. It further allows you to cater to your clients' evolving needs as they respond to these changes in the marketplace.

In summary, continuous learning in digital marketing is similar to navigating a mighty river. While the currents shift and change, your ability to adapt and learn is like adjusting your sails to maintain the correct course. Ignoring these changes may lead to becoming stagnant or even lost in your marketing approaches. Therefore, staying up-to-date, constantly evolving with the market trends, practicing continuous learning and embracing changes are not only essential but vital for achieving sustained success in your digital marketing journey. As a freelancer, you must become a master of this art of remaining relevant in this ever-evolving digital world.